Let's Plant a Garden

By Karen Sontag

W9-BIC-828

Scott Foresman
is an imprint of

PEARSON

Glenview, Illinois • Boston, Massachusetts • Chandler, Arizona •
Upper Saddle River, New Jersey

Photographs

Every effort has been made to secure permission and provide appropriate credit for photographic material. The publisher deeply regrets any omission and pledges to correct errors called to its attention in subsequent editions.

Unless otherwise acknowledged, all photographs are the property of Pearson Education, Inc.

Photo locators denoted as follows: Top (T), Center (C), Bottom (B), Left (L), Right (R), Background (Bkgd)

Opener: ©Tony Anderson/Getty Images; **1** ©Jim West/Alamy Images; **3** ©Digital Vision Ltd./SuperStock; **4** ©Jim West/Alamy Images; **5** ©Jim West/Alamy Images; **6** ©norr/Shutterstock; **7** ©Tony Anderson/Getty Images; **8** ©Henry Georgi/Aurora/Getty Images.

ISBN 13: 978-0-328-46306-0
ISBN 10:   0-328-46306-X

10 11 V010 17 16 15 14

Someone has an idea.
We can have a garden!

Someone brings some dirt.
We can dig the garden.

Someone brings some seeds.
We can plant the garden.

Someone brings some water.

We can water the garden.

Someone brings some gloves.
We can weed the garden.

Someone brings a camera.
We can remember our garden!

Think and Share

Read Together

1. What idea did someone have?

2. What are some different ways people helped?

3. What other projects could a school or neighborhood do?

Science

Concept Literacy
Leveled Reader

Genre	Concept
Nonfiction	Ideas That Change Our World

Scott Foresman Reading Street   1.5.6

Scott Foresman
is an imprint of

ISBN-13: 978-0-328-46306-0
ISBN-10:   0-328-46306-X